# Sailing For Beginners
## Instruction to Sailing for Beginners

Copyright © 2020

All rights reserved.

**DEDICATION**

The author and publisher have provided this e-book to you for your personal use only. You may not make this e-book publicly available in any way. Copyright infringement is against the law. If you believe the copy of this e-book you are reading infringes on the author's copyright, please notify the publisher at: https://us.macmillan.com/piracy

# Contents

What Is Sailing? ...................................................................... 1

Apparent Wind Velocity .......................................................... 5

Lift and Drag on Sails ............................................................. 9

4 Benefits of Sailing ............................................................. 12

Different Types of Sailing .................................................... 17

Basics of Sailing ................................................................... 30

10 Tips for Sailing Beginners ............................................... 37

# What Is Sailing?

Sailing employs the wind—acting on sails, wingsails or kites—to propel a craft on the surface of the water (sailing ship, sailboat, windsurfer, or kitesurfer), on ice (iceboat) or on land (land yacht) over a chosen course, which is often part of a larger plan of navigation.

# History

Throughout history sailing has been instrumental in the development of civilization, affording humanity greater mobility than travel over land, whether for trade, transport or warfare, and the capacity for fishing. The earliest representation of a ship under sail appears on a painted disc found in Kuwait dating between 5500 and 5000 BCE. They would go selling and teaching other civilizations how to build, sail and navigate the ships. Austronesian oceanfarers traveled vast distances of open ocean in outrigger canoes using navigation methods such as stick charts. Advances in sailing technology from the Middle Ages onward enabled Arab, Chinese, Indian and European explorers to make longer voyages into regions with extreme weather and climatic conditions. There were improvements in sails, masts and rigging; improvements in marine navigation, including the cross tree and charts of both the sea and constellations, allowed more certainty in sea travel. From the 15th century onwards,

European ships went further north, stayed longer on the Grand Banks and in the Gulf of St. Lawrence, and eventually began to explore the Pacific Northwest and the Western Arctic. Sailing has contributed to many great explorations in the world.

According to Jett, the Egyptians used a bipod mast to support a sail that allowed a reed craft to travel upriver with a following wind, as late as 3,500 BCE. Such sails evolved into the square-sail rig that persisted up to the 19th century. Such rigs generally could not sail much closer than 80° to the wind. Fore-and-aft rigs appear to have evolved in Southeast Asia—dates are uncertain—allowing for rigs that could sail as close as 60–75° off the wind.

## Physics

The physics of sailing arises from a balance of forces between the wind powering the sailing craft as it passes over its sails and the resistance by the sailing craft against being blown off course, which is provided in the water by the keel, rudder, underwater foils and other elements of the underbody of a sailboat, on ice by the runners of an ice boat, or on land by the wheels of a sail-powered land vehicle.

**Apparent Wind Velocity**

Forces on sails depend on wind speed and direction and the speed and direction of the craft. The speed of the craft at a given point of sail contributes to the "apparent wind"—the wind speed and direction as measured on the moving craft. The apparent wind on the sail creates a total aerodynamic force, which may be resolved into drag—the force component in the direction of the apparent wind—and lift—the force component normal (90°) to the apparent wind. Depending on the alignment of the sail with the apparent wind (angle of attack), lift or drag may be the predominant propulsive component. Depending on the angle of attack of a set of sails with respect to the apparent wind, each sail is providing motive force to the sailing craft either from lift-dominant attached flow or drag-dominant separated flow. Additionally, sails may interact with one another to create forces that are different from the sum of the individual contributions of each sail, when used alone.

The term "velocity" refers both to speed and direction. As applied to wind, apparent wind velocity (VA) is the air velocity acting upon the leading edge of the most forward sail or as experienced by instrumentation or crew on a moving sailing craft. In nautical terminology, wind speeds are normally expressed in knots and wind angles in degrees. All sailing craft reach a constant forward velocity (VB) for a given true wind velocity (VT) and point of sail. The craft's point of sail affects its velocity for a given true wind velocity. Conventional sailing craft cannot derive power from the wind in a "no-go" zone that is approximately 40° to 50° away from the true wind, depending on the craft. Likewise, the directly downwind speed of all conventional sailing craft is limited to the true wind speed. As a sailboat sails further from the wind, the apparent wind becomes smaller and the lateral component becomes less; boat speed is highest on the beam reach. In order to act like an airfoil, the sail on a sailboat is sheeted further out as the course is further off the wind. As an iceboat sails further from the wind, the apparent wind increases slightly and the boat speed is highest on the broad reach. In order to act like an airfoil, the sail on an iceboat is sheeted in for all three points of sail.

## Lift and Drag on Sails

Lift on a sail, acting as an airfoil, occurs in a direction perpendicular to the incident airstream (the apparent wind velocity for the head sail) and is a result of pressure differences between the windward and leeward surfaces and depends on angle of attack, sail shape, air density, and speed of the apparent wind. The lift force results from the average pressure on the windward surface of the sail being higher than the average pressure on the leeward side. These pressure differences arise in conjunction with the curved air flow. As air follows a curved path along the windward side of a sail, there is a pressure gradient perpendicular to the flow direction with higher pressure on the outside of the curve and lower pressure on the inside. To generate lift, a sail must present an "angle of attack" between the chord line of the sail and the apparent wind velocity. Angle of attack is a function of both the craft's point of sail and how the sail is adjusted with respect to the apparent wind.

As the lift generated by a sail increases, so does lift-induced drag, which together with parasitic drag constitute total drag, which acts in a direction parallel to the incident airstream. This occurs as the angle of attack increases with sail trim or change of course and causes the lift coefficient to increase up to the point of aerodynamic stall along with the lift-induced drag coefficient. At the onset of stall, lift is abruptly decreased, as is lift-induced drag. Sails with the apparent wind behind them (especially going downwind) operate in a stalled condition.

Lift and drag are components of the total aerodynamic force on sail, which are resisted by forces in the water (for a boat) or on the traveled surface (for an ice boat or land sailing craft). Sails act in two basic modes; under the lift-predominant mode, the sail behaves in a manner analogous to a wing with airflow attached to both surfaces; under the drag-predominant mode, the sail acts in a manner analogous to a parachute with airflow in detached flow, eddying around the sail.

# 4 Benefits of Sailing

Embarking on a journey at sea can be an arduous task, especially when you are competing in a race for glory. But when the stakes aren't high and you've got no competition, the sport can be extremely rewarding and beneficial to your health. Although considered an extreme sport, sailing has often been used as an escape for those with busy schedules and stressed-out minds, or just a means to get a fresh breath of air. While indulging in the ecstasy of sailing, here are some of its other benefits:

# 1. Increased Immune System

Exposure to challenging weather for at least three to four hours daily can significantly improve your immune system. This is because your body will recalibrate itself to be able to withstand erratic climates, building a new and stronger defence mechanism. In that sense, unpredictable weather is a friend of the sailor. From soaking up more than enough vitamin D one minute to getting showered in rain and salt the next, sailors become harder to take down than the average person when it comes to getting sick.

## 2. Decision-Making & Other Mental Skills

Sailing isn't just steering the boat to where you want to go; it's also pre-empting the challenges you may face during the journey. To excel on the sea, you have to be able to understand and read the environment around you. Making split-second decisions becomes second-nature and will help increase your mental capacity and thought process on land. Sailing also requires a lot of concentration and mindfulness. So if you find that you are often distracted from tasks, sailing might be the therapy you need to instil efficiency in your life.

## 3. Organisational Skills

Being organised is useful everywhere and believe it or not, sailing is a place where you can hone this skill. It's inherent to follow procedures and keep things neat and orderly, or "shipshape", in order for the boat to function systematically and without error. Have an organisation problem at work or at home? Sailing will make you unable to live in mess and disarray.

## 4. Escapism & Relaxation

Sailing is just relaxing, period. The sun rays hitting your skin on a nice afternoon in the bay, birds flying past, fishes dancing in the water beneath you—these are just some of the natural therapeutics sensations that can be experienced when you're out in the water in a swiftly moving boat. For some people, a hobby like sailing can be their only time in a week to be alone and away from the noise of urban life. Tune out of the world and literally escape out to sea.

# Different Types of Sailing

## 1. Fleet Racing

Fleet racing can be either 'one-design' or 'handicap'. One design racing, as at the Olympic Sailing Competition means that boats racing against each other are all the same - the same design, the same sail area etc. Handicap racing means different types of boat can race against each other. Each boat has a handicap or rating so that their finish times can be adjusted or their start time determined so that the slowest boats go first.

Fleet racing can be any length of time with several taking place in a day or as a round the world race such as the Volvo Ocean Race.

Sailing For Beginners

## 2. Match Racing

A match racing course is always a windward / leeward course and each race takes approximately 20 minutes to complete.

A match race begins four minutes before the starting time when each boat must enter the starting area from opposite ends of the start line. As soon as they enter the starting area they will engage in a pre-start battle as each one tries to gain an avantage over the other. They will both be trying to cause the other boat to infringe a rule and so receive a penalty or to simply get the most advantageous position on the starting line for themselves so they are in control of the race.

Match racing is officiated by umpires on the water who follow the boats and make instant on-course decisions about whether a penalty is given. The umpire boat will use yellow and blue flags to indicate which boat has been given a penalty or a green flag if no penalty is given.

When a boat is penalized it must complete a full circle penalty turn. This can be done at any time during the race before the finish line. If one boat has a penalty and the other also gets one before the first has taken theirs then they are cancelled out. If a boat receives three penalties then it is disqualified.

## 3. Team Racing

Team Racing typically consists of two teams each of three boats competing against each other. It is a fast paced racing style which depends on excellent boat handling skills and rapid tactical decision making.

The teams will race to try and achieve a winning combination of places - the lowest score wins. The scoring system is 1 for first place, 2 for second and so on. If one boat in the team wins the race they are not guaranteed glory as their combined score must be ten or less to win - 2,3,5 = 10 points v 1,4,6 = 11 points

If a team is lying in 1,4,6 then the boat in first place will go back and try to help his team mates through to 2,3,5 or better. How does he do this?

A team racer has two main weapons. Firstly, he can position his boat between the wind and his opponent, thus blanketing his sails and slowing him down. Secondly he can use the right of way rules to his advantage, approaching his opponent in such as way that his adversary has to change course or incur a penalty. Both these weapons are deployed before the start when the manoeuvres begin, with all six boats performing an intricate and aggressive dance to try and gain the advantage.

The racing is followed by umpires on the water who issue on the spot penalties. If a boat is protested agains by another boat they can accept it and perform a 360 degree penalty turn straight away or wait for the umpires to give a decision which may result in a green flag (no penalty) or a 720 degree turn.

# 4. Offshore & Oceanic Sailing

There are many types of Oceanic and Offshore racing events which are organized for one design classes as well as handicap or rating systems. In order to achieve an orderly schedule, World Sailing works with event organizers to monitor the calendar of events.

The differences between the types of oceanic and offshore racing, ranging from trans-oceanic racing to short-course day races sailed in protected waters, are reflected in the six categories of the World Sailing Offshore Special Regulations which provide for the differences in the minimum standards of safety and accommodation.

## 5. Para World Sailing

Whatever your background, sailing is a versatile sport that can accommodate many types of disability. The first step is to find out what is already happening in your area by contacing the World Sailing Member National Authority (MNA) or Para Sports Organization in your country or simply visiting a local sailing club.

Almost any boat can be sailed by people with disabilities although it is clear that some are more suitable than others.

In 1996 sailing was included on the programme of the Paralympic Games as a demonstration event and it has been full medal sport until the Rio 2016 Para Games. It is one of the only sports in the Para sports in which athletes of any disability compete together.

# 6. Cruising

Cruising is arguably the most commonly enjoyed sailing discipline and through it's responsibility to all areas of the sport, World Sailing works with a number of organizations to defend boater rights.

Cruising can be a coastal day sail or a longer distance international journeys crossing oceans and national borders.

World Sailing works with organizations such as the International Maritime Organization and the International Organization for Standardization to represent the interests of sailors worldwide.

The Piracy updates and links in the Safety section are essential reading for sailors considering cruising in certain waters.

# 10 Nautical & Sailing Terms To Know

**1. Aft** - The back of a ship. If something is located aft, it is at the back of the sailboat. The aft is also known as the stern.

**2. Bow** - The front of the ship is called the bow. Knowing the location of the bow is important for defining two of the other most common sailing terms: port (left of the bow) and starboard (right of the bow).

**3. Port** - Port is always the left-hand side of the boat when you are facing the bow. Because "right" and "left" can become confusing sailing terms when used out in the open waters, port is used to define the left-hand side of the boat as it relates to the bow, or front.

**4. Starboard** - Starboard is always the right-hand side of the boat when you are facing the bow. Because "right" and "left" can become confusing sailing terms when used out in the open waters, starboard is used to define the right-hand side of the boat as it relates to the bow, or front.

**5. Leeward** - Also known as lee, leeward is the direction opposite to the way the wind is currently blowing (windward).

**6. Windward** - The direction in which the wind is currently blowing. Windward is the opposite of leeward (the opposite direction of the wind). Sailboats tend to move with the wind, making the windward direction an important sailing term to know.

**7. Boom** - The boom is the horizontal pole which extends from the bottom of the mast. Adjusting the boom towards the direction of the wind is how the sailboat is able to harness wind power in order to move forward or backwards.

**8. Rudder** - Located beneath the boat, the rudder is a flat piece of wood, fiberglass, or metal that is used to steer the ship. Larger sailboats control the rudder via a wheel, while smaller sailboats will have a steering mechanism directly aft.

**9. Tacking** - The opposite of jibing, this basic sailing maneuver refers to turning the bow of the boat through the wind so that the wind changes from one side of the boat to the other side. The boom of a boat will always shift from one side to the other when performing a tack or a jibe.

**10. Jibing** - The opposite of tacking, this basic sailing maneuver refers to turning the stern of the boat through the wind so that the wind changes from one side of the boat to the other side. The boom of a boat will always shift from one side to the other when performing a tack or a jibe. Jibing is a less common technique than tacking, since it involves turning a boat directly into the wind.

# Basics of Sailing

## Points of Sail

These are basically the directions a sailboat can and cannot maneuver and the accompanying sail positions that make it happen. Terms such as beam, broad and close reach describe at which angle the wind is contacting the boat and therefore how to adjust the sails for peak performance. You'll learn that with the wind straight on the bow, you may end up "in irons", which is the no go zone.

## Parts of the Boat

Learn the unique parts of a boat so you'll know what to touch, look at or do when the instructor in your first class gives you a directive. For example, understanding "ease the jib sheet" or "luff the main" could save you from getting very wet on your first day. Boat parts have unique names like vang, downhaul, mizzen, centerboard, boltrope, the luff and leech of a sail, and so forth. Once you learn that there are no ropes on a boat (only "lines"), you'll sound like a pro too.

## Sailing Videos, Online Classes, Sailing Schools

Instructional videos on YouTube or other sources will help you connect the terminology with the reality. The first day on a sailboat can be overwhelming so the more you know beforehand, the less stressed you'll be.

You can learn to sail without lessons, but professional instruction will make it a lot faster and you'll learn the right way to do things. Start on a small boat where the equipment is simple and cause-and-effect is clear because your actions provide immediate feedback. Beginning on a tiller (rather than a wheel) boat usually creates sailors who are more in tune with a vessel later on. The first day of class, you'll learn to "rig" (put together) the boat, basic maneuvering (tacking, gybing and docking) and baseline safety issues.

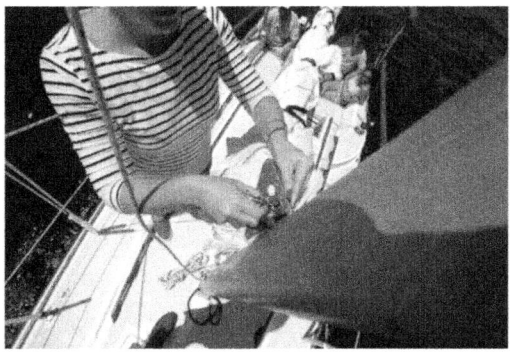

## Knot Tying

There are many "lines" on a boat and therefore many knots in use. Knowing how to tie at least a handful of them will help you manage the boat better and that includes knowing how to tie on fenders and attaching a line to a cleat once you're at the dock. Knot tying is an activity you can perfect in your spare time when not on the water.

## Sail Trim

Sailing well is all about sail trim, which is the way the sails are used and shaped. Easing (letting out) and trimming (hauling in) the sails will make a big difference in how you sail. When sailing upwind, you'll want the sails tight or flat but when sailing down or off the wind, you'll want them to be curved and full to catch as much air (wind) as possible.

The basic theory is clear-cut but the application of that knowledge can take years to perfect. You'll soon learn to use telltales (strings of yarn attached to the jib and mainsail) to help you see what the apparent wind is doing and how to use it to your advantage. Sails are airfoils and sailing is about geometry and physics. Although you don't need to be a mathematician or physicist to sail, understating concepts like the "centers of effort and lateral resistance" will help the pieces of the puzzle fall into place.

## Rules of the Road

Finally, you'll need to know how to interact with other boat traffic on the water. Understanding who is under obligation to move will help you avoid a collision. Those with the right of way are called the "stand-on" vessel while the others are the "give way" vessel. The rules are based on the type of boat (sail, power or human propelled), the location of the interaction (restricted channels or open water) and the activity the boats are involved in at the point of potential encounter (like sailing, fishing or towing). Regardless of the rules, the objective is to avoid a collision at all costs so you should never insist on your rights regardless of the circumstances.

Learning to sail is just the beginning of a lifetime of enjoyment, especially if you're bitten by the sailing bug so enjoy the process from the rudimentary basics to the subtle nuances that will make you an expert.

# Frequently Asked Questions about Sailing

## Why should I learn to sail?

After learning to sail you can decide to compete in Club racing or just cruise around Carlingford Lough. Racing is great fun and you will find a warm and friendly welcome when you join the Club for its twice-weekly racing. Alternatively you may wish to cruise around and admire the beauty of Carlingford Lough.

## What do I need to get started?

Nothing, just book a learner course and you will be given the training needed to sail safely on Carlingford Lough.

## Do I have to get wet?

Not if you don't want to. You can choose to learn on a keelboat rather than a dinghy. However dinghies are more fun.

## When can I do it?

 Any time that suits you. The weekends are best as you have 2 intense days of training to get going or you may prefer evening lessons instead. It's up to you.

## Is it safe?

As a Royal Yachting Association approved Training Centre, CLYC places a major emphasis on safety. You will also have a fully qualified instructor with you and you will be wearing a buoyancy aid at all times.

## Do I need my own boat?

No, a boat can be rented for your training course.

## Is sailing an expensive sport?

No, you can pick up a starter boat for as little as £250 or you can crew on a boat without having to spend any money at all. Club membership fees are comparatively low for full sailing membership for a year. Members can hire a dinghy from the club for a year at attractive rates, which include insurance and parking fees.

## What age do I have to be?

Any age – you are never too old to learn, as long as you are agile enough to jump in and out of a boat.

## After doing a sailing course how do I continue to sail?

Most people will join a sailing club in order to develop the skills that they have learned on their course. CLYC Killowen is actively looking for new members and you will receive a friendly welcome.

# 10 Tips for Sailing Beginners

## 1. Get to Grips with Basic Sailing Terms

Before you hit the water, make sure you've read up on some of the basic sailing terms you'll need. Being familiar with these terms will enable an instructor to impart information to you more easily, meaning that you'll really get the most out of your sessions.

## 2. Take Instruction

Don't try and teach yourself on the water. Not only is this dangerous, it is also likely to be a time consuming and therefore costly. By all means invest some time learning the basics from guides and books, but practical instruction should come from someone with good sailing experience. A good sailing course is worth investing in.

## 3.   Start in Calm, Uncrowded Waters

One of the best tips for sailing beginners we can give is to start out in calm and quiet waters. Nobody wants to be starting out in rough open waters or surrounded by boats containing skilled yachtsmen who clearly know what they are doing. If you're just starting to master the basics, then start out in conditions where winds are light and traffic is low. A contained marina is perhaps the safest option.

## 4.   Start Small

Like no-one chooses to learn to drive using a bus, the same applies to sailing. Start with a small boat, ideally a small dinghy. This will be much more responsive and easy to manoeuvre. It will also be far easier to deal with in the event of capsizing, which you will inevitably do as some point.

## 5. Check Conditions

Once you are ready to go out alone, it always pays to check conditions beforehand. Check information concerning tides, wind and weather conditions so that you are prepared for whatever may come your way. Be sure to have the right gear and provisions as required.

## 6. Capsize!

No we're not crazy, but you really need to have practised how to deal with your boat capsizing. It is better to do this within a controlled environment where there is help at hand, rather than confronting this eventuality when you are in open water. Trust us, you will capsize at some point, so a test-capsize is essential.

## 7. Boom or Bust

Watch out for the boom – the horizontal pole that extends from the bottom of a mast – as it can cause injury or even send you overboard.

The boom is most commonly responsible for onboard injuries, so always keep a watch for when the boom is about to swing. It might just save you a major headache or worse.

## 8. Safety First

Your safety is of paramount importance. No matter what your level of experience there are certain safety precautions that should always apply. These include informing people of your intention to head out on the water, wearing a floatation jacket, and of course, being able to swim.

## 9. Know the Right-of-Way

It's not a sailing free-for-all out there – there are rules to govern how sailing craft should manoeuvre to ensure they do not collide with one another. How you move is based on many variables including what side the wind is on, what type of craft it is, whether you are planning to overtake. Get familiar with these nautical rules to prevent mishap.

## 10. Always Maintain A Lookout

It may seem obvious, but always look where you are going! Sailing is fun but there are plenty of other craft out there, so maintain a proper lookout using both your eyes and ears to help prevent collisions. To give you sufficient time to respond to danger you should always maintain a safe speed.

# Types of Sailboats and Their Uses

## 1. Beach Catamaran

These are generally 14–20 feet in length primarily used for daysailing. They are fast boats that require some agility to sail. They have shallow drafts when the dagger boards are up for beaching.

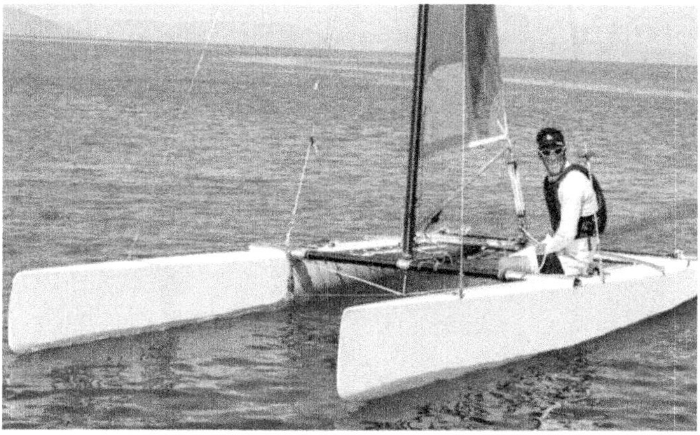

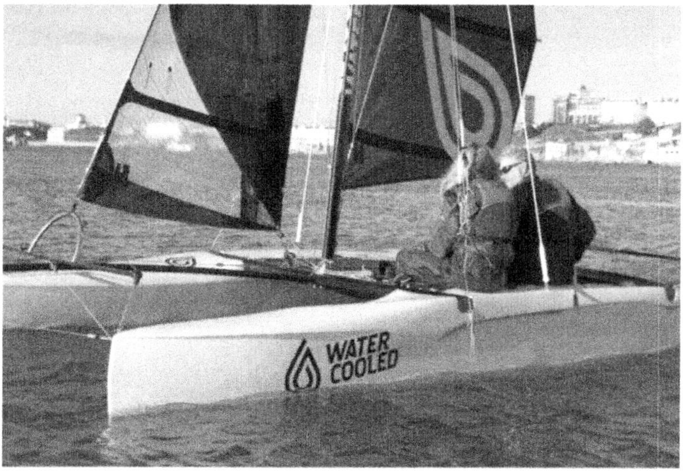
WATER
COOLED

## 2. Cruising Catamaran

A larger relative of the beach catamaran, they share more in common with a cruising mono-hull with accommodation for extended cruising. They are stable platforms with shallow drafts and are 25–50+ feet in length.

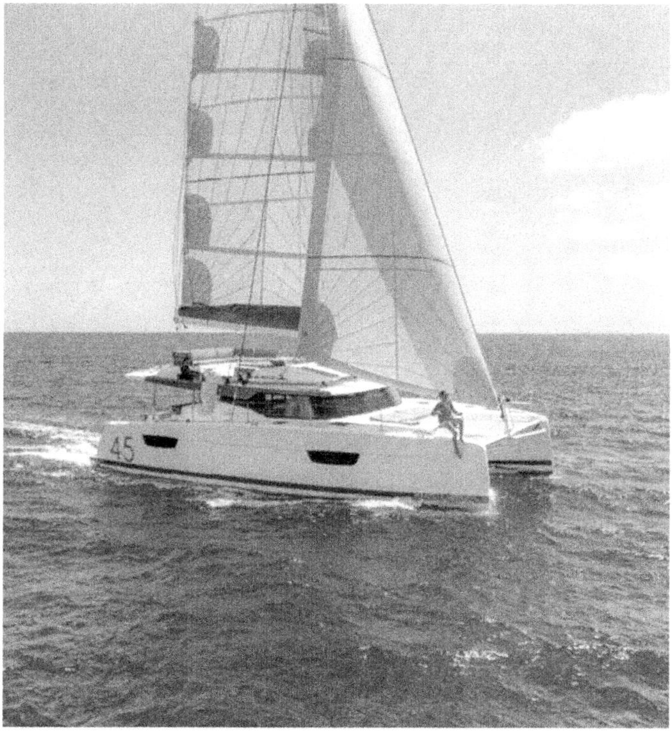
45

Sailing For Beginners

## 3. Cruising Sailboat

Generally 16–50+ feet in length, these boats are cabins for extended cruising. Boats larger than 26 feet usually have standing headroom down below. Many of the more popular models have large fleets and are raced or have fleet associations for group cruising.

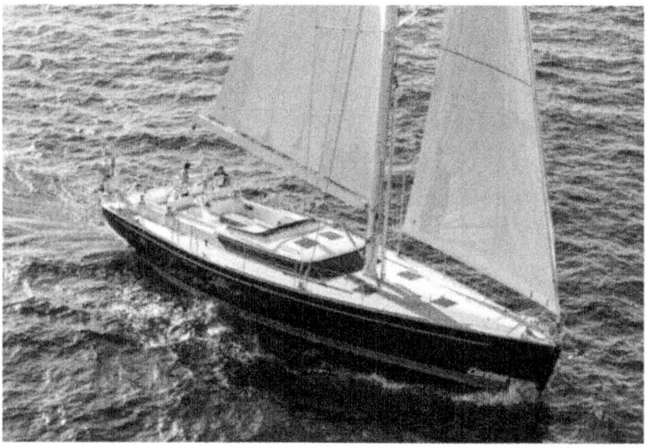

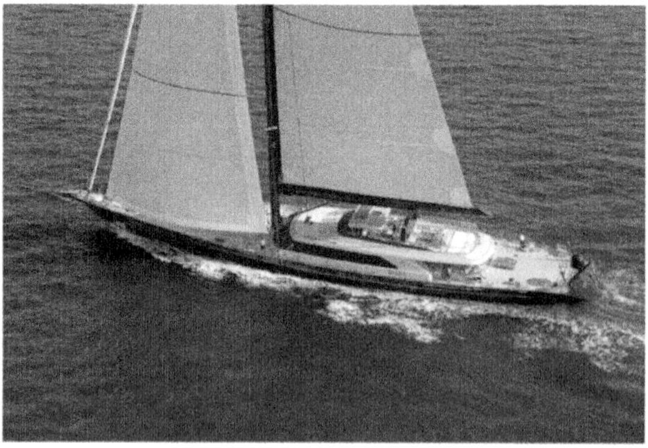

## 4. Daysailer

These boats are generally 14–20 feet in length. They can seat up to 4 passengers. As the name implied they are intended for day use with a small cuddy cabin for storing gear. Many can accommodate a small outboard. They make a great choice for new boaters.

Sailing For Beginners

## 5. Motorsailer

Motorsailers are sailboats powered with inboard engines allowing long cruises under power or sail. They have luxury accommodations and usually 35 feet and over. They are a compromise giving up sailing speed due to a smaller rig and added weight for the engine and larger gas and water tanks.

Sailing For Beginners

## 6. Racer-Cruiser

This is a hybrid of the cruising boat built to accommodate overnight cruising but trimmed with the equipment for competitive racing. They are generally 25 feet and over.

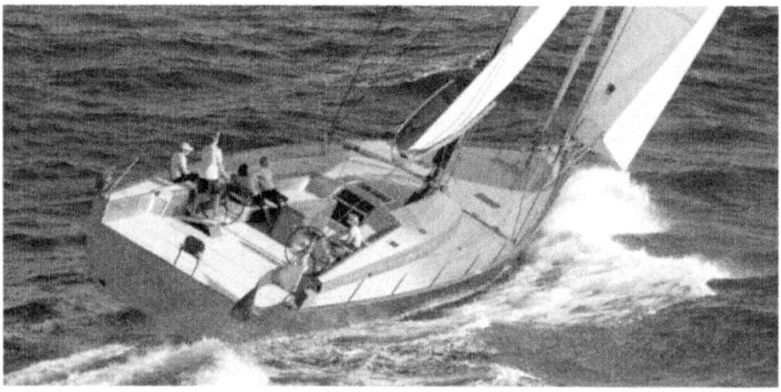

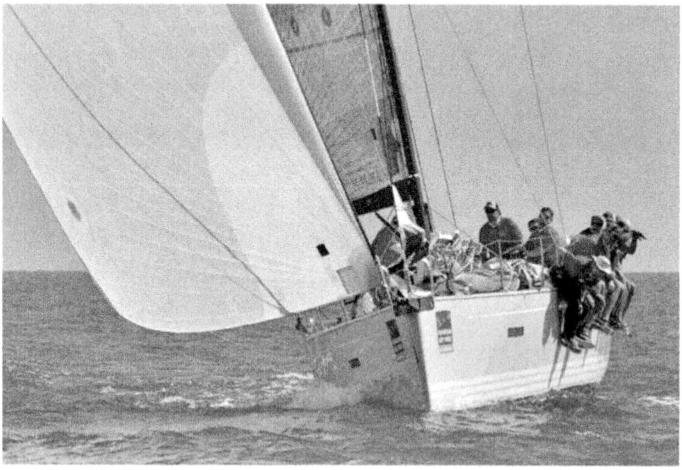

## 7. Racing Sailboats

Similar to cruising boats but have more equipment and are built lighter, with spartan accommodations. They are not intended to be a comfortable ride, just a fast one. Usually 20–70+ feet in length. Just as these are related to cruising boats, there are smaller, faster cousins of sailing dinghies that are also raced.

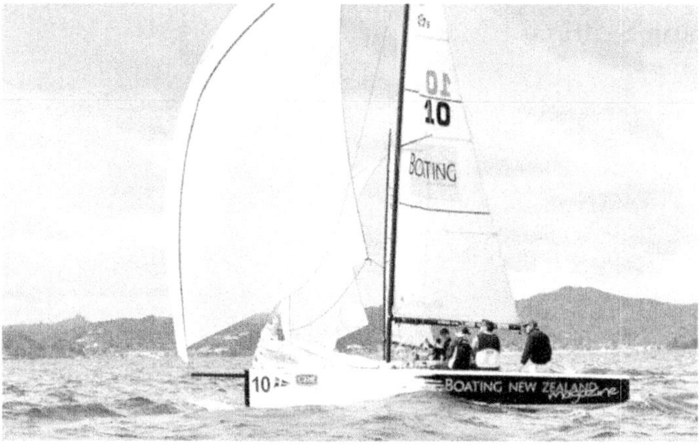
10
BOATING NEW ZEALAND

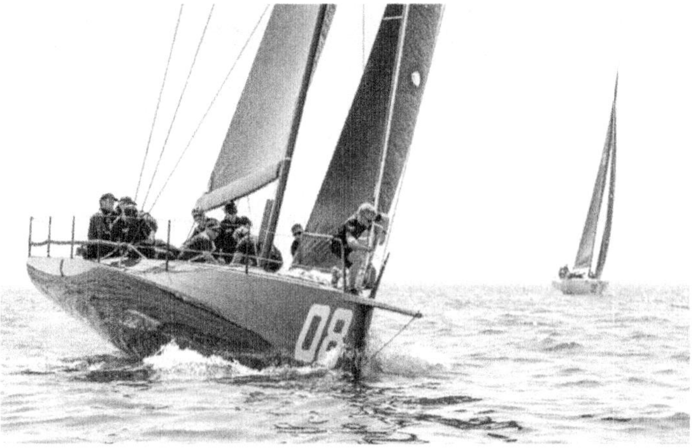
08

## 8. Sailing Dinghies

Small (under 15 feet) these boats are usually one or two person boats. These are boats that guarantee a wet ride. Many are competitively raced. They are a great choice for those that are new to boating.

Sailing For Beginners

# Sailing For Beginners

# Sailing For Beginners